New Iri... Scr...

The Galty, Knockmealdown and Comeragh Mountains
40 Walks and Scrambles

Dedicated to the memory of
Willie Rattray, climber and scientist

Willie Rattray died from injuries received in a climbing accident in early August 1997 on Mont Maudit in Chamonix, France. He was 29. A scientist by profession, Willie joined UCC Mountaineering Club in his first year at college and became an avid walker, climber and alpinist. A veteran of many trips to Scotland and Wales with UCC, he departed to Edmonton in Canada to undertake a PhD in Food Science and to continue his climbing career. His regular postcards kept us informed of his trips to the big mountains of the Canadian Rockies and during this time he also managed to fit in an Alpine season in Europe. His return to Ireland in early 1998 to take up a research post meant a return to the hills of Ireland and the countryside that he loved. His death in the Alps came as a great shock to all his friends in the climbing community.

Willie Rattray loved life and nature and like many of us, cared little for the badges and trappings of success. He was content to be himself. I dedicate this book to his memory, and remember the echoes of his passing. *Ar dheis de go raibh a anam.*

THE GALTY, KNOCKMEALDOWN AND COMERAGH MOUNTAINS
40 WALKS AND SCRAMBLES

Barry Keane

THE COLLINS PRESS

Published by The Collins Press, Carey's Lane, The Huguenot Quarter, Cork 1998

British Library Cataloguing in Publication data.

Printed in Ireland by Colour Books Ltd., Dublin

Jacket design by Upper Case Ltd., Cornmarket Street, Cork

ISBN: 1-898256-48-9

CONTENTS

SECTION III: SLIEVENAMON

SECTION IV: THE GALTY AND BALLYHOURA MOUNTAINS

ACKNOWLEDGEMENTS

This is the fourth book in the series of walking and scrambling guides. I never imagined that things would have progressed this far. I owe a great debt of thanks to my friends who not only did the routes for and with me, but have also bought the guides!

The main contributors to the guides include Brian Girvan and Dan Cahill, whose name was omitted from the other three guides due to the rush to get them published. Likewise, I also omitted Tim Cotter, who not only climbed many of the routes with me, but was great at spotting the best line. Besides these two gents, the usual suspects from the Cork and Kerry climbing community can take much of the blame. If I have left anyone out, I apologise now.

My long-standing proof-reader and foil, Henry O'Keeffe, has again done the honours and brought the text to somewhere approaching reality.

I hope that the people using the guides will find them of use and I am always willing to listen to any suggestions or answer any queries that people may have.

Barry Keane

1. ACCOMMODATION

Bord Fáilte (the Irish Tourist Board) can cater for all your needs from Five Star hotels to Bed and Breakfasts. They also produce an excellent guide to self-catering accommodation. Self-catering is relatively cheap outside the summer months and Irish Bank Holiday weekends. An Óige (Irish Youth Hostels) have some lovely hostels right in the mountains including Mountain Lodge in the Galty Mountains which is powered entirely by gas. Independent Hostels are dotted all over the southeast, and many are into the outdoor scene or will have information on the local hillwalking clubs.

2. MAPS

The new Ordnance Survey 1:50,000 maps cover the Galty Mountains, the Knockmealdowns and the Comeraghs. These are essential for anyone intending to venture into the Irish hills. The sketch maps in the guide are precisely that, and are intended only as general location maps for the hills. See also Weather and Safety. Ordnance Survey maps 74 and 75 cover the area.

3. ACCESS

I have never encountered access problems in these mountains. However, the farmers are especially sensitive about dogs on their hills and prefer if you leave them behind. Traditionally, climbers, hillwalkers and farmers have always got on and it is usual to stop for a chat if you meet someone. Despite this, in the hills of the southeast, it is rare to meet any of the farmers, unlike the hills of the southwest. Usually the main problem is trying to decide which dubious track or firebreak will lead you on or off the hills through the forestry.

4. GRADINGS

In the series, a total of 12 different grades are used. Five of these are for hillwalking, five for scrambling and 2 are for scrambling/rockclimbing. Hopefully, these give a good guide as to the length or overall difficulty of a day out. The grades in the guide are based on personal experience and the views of mountaineers who have either done the routes with me or followed my suggestions as to which climb is where.

Hillwalk 1: These are easy half day walks with no problems other than very minor navigational ones. Excellent as a quick stroll after tea or as a brief introduction to hillwalking.

Hillwalk 2: Longer walks with no rough ground and few if any other problems. Good family days out as long as someone can navigate and people have the minimum of equipment, like proper boots.

Hillwalk 3: Your normal day out with some steep or rough ground requiring reasonable mountain skills and a good knowledge of how to navigate using maps and compass.

Hillwalk 4: Long day walks requiring good fitness, good navigation skills, especially in misty conditions and generally good mountain skills.

Hillwalk 5: Multi-day walks for backpackers or those with a week to spend. Involving good fitness and stamina, good map reading and navigation skills and a generally good understanding of the mountain environment in all conditions.

Scramble 1: Easy scrambling on hillwalks, most of which can be avoided if you wish. A good introduction to the most interesting and potentially dangerous of games that climbers play. A rope is rarely necessary but should be available if someone loses their nerve. Usually easy to retreat down or left or right to easier ground.

Scramble 2: More scrambling, slightly steeper with less options to avoid everything.

Scramble 3: More committing but easy to retreat either left or right to easier ground. Vegetation or loose rock may be a problem. The odd easy rock-climbing move will present itself.

Scramble 4: Generally easy to moderate rockclimbing with harder options usually available. The scrambling line always takes the line of least resistance. Vegetation or loose rock may be a problem.

Scramble 5: Committing climbs generally of moderate climbing with moves up to difficult presenting themselves. Usually very exposed or in gullies. Wet rock, vegetation or loose rock may add to the difficulties.

Scramble 6/Rock 1: Sustained, wet, loose and hard climbs generally difficult on buttresses with some very difficult moves. Using the rope is advisable unless you are very competent or confident.

Scramble 7/Rock 2: Mainly rockclimbing routes which are technically challenging with moves up to and including severe, and a rope, climbing gear and ability are more than advisable.

NB. Add one grade if the rock is wet. As the rock can be loose especially in the Comeraghs, it should be treated with caution, and when in doubt, use the rope.

5a. DISTANCES AND TIMINGS OF WALKS

All distances are in metres (m) or kilometres (km) as appropriate, and the total distance is given from start to finish of the day. The scrambles only take up a small part of the day out.

b. HEIGHTS

All heights are given in metres (m) and the height gain is the total ascent for the day, give or take a few metres.

c. Time
This is a rough guide based on 15 minutes per kilometre and 3 minutes per 30 metres, which has served me well in the southeast. Rests are not included so these should be added to the overall time. Fit groups will have no bother in beating the guidebook time, but they might not enjoy the view!

6. Route Number and Name
Each route is numbered and given a name. In many cases, these names may not be known to some climbers as the new maps have either relocated or not named well-known land marks in the hills. Among climbers, names drift between English and Irish, but usually this is not insurmountable. I have used the names on the 1:50,000 maps, and noted other names if I thought it would assist the reader.

7. Route Description
I have tried to include the main features of all routes, but what I find significant may not be to the person on the route. Some people may find the descriptions terse, but if I included every last detail it would reduce the spirit of adventure and discovery to an unacceptable level. As a general rule the scrambles go straight up from the bottom of the route with little traversing left or

right. I must emphasise that it is up to the person climbing the route to use their common sense. All gully routes stay in the gully unless otherwise mentioned.

8. WEATHER

Like any mountain area in Ireland or the British Isles, the weather is constantly changing. However, these hills lie in the path of the southwesterlies and massive amounts of rain combined with gale force winds can sweep in from the Atlantic almost without warning. The weather forecast can be wrong on many occasions but they usually get rain spreading from the west spot on. Galtymore is subject to extremely high winds and these mountains tend to get and hold snow more than their cousins in the southwest.

9. SAFETY

Anyone going into the Irish hills at any time must be in the company of someone who can navigate, or can navigate themselves. This is not an optional extra. No guidebook can hope to get you up and down a mountain route in safety – it can only suggest options and possibilities. After that you are entirely on your own.

You must also have the correct equipment; rain gear, food, spare clothing, a first-aid kit and rudimentary bivouac equipment are essential items. Rock climbing equipment should always be brought along by scramblers just in case but you don't need a great amount.

The extreme changeability of the weather means that you should always have a good idea of the weather forecast and be willing to turn back if the weather is too bad.

A basic knowledge of first-aid is also something that is needed, as help can be many hours away, and it may well be up to you to keep someone alive.

An understanding of winter climbing when snow lies on the hills is also a vital requirement Some of the most horrible accidents occur to people who slipped on a patch of snow, and were not able to stop themselves from falling. Scramblers should have a knowledge of basic rope techniques and enough rock climbing knowledge to belay someone safely up or down a route.

Remember there are few, if any tracks in the Irish hills, and very few people, so you are on your own most of the time. This puts a greater responsibility on the mountaineer to be self sufficient, but also allows you much greater freedom. All of this can be learn by osmosis in your local mountaineering or hillwalking club, but once you have the basics you can discover the hills for yourself.

10. EQUIPMENT

The essential item of equipment for a scrambler is a pair of 3 season mountaineering boots with at least a three-quarter shank. For hillwalking you can purchase an ordinary pair of walking boots with good weatherproofing and good protection for the ankle. After that you will need raingear, a rope, some slings a minimal amount of rock climbing equipment and a rucksack narrow enough to fit pour back.

11. RESCUE

Call the Gardaí if you have a problem and they will alert the rescue services for you. Remember that it may take at least a couple of hours for the rescue team to get to you.

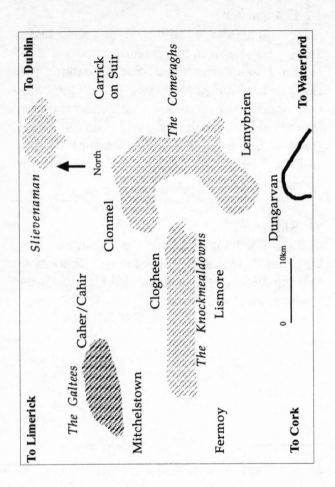

16

Introduction

From the Skelligs, two superb seastacks almost battered into submission by the Atlantic, the Amorician folding extends in a broad sweep over 200km as far east as Dungarvan in west Waterford. The first three books in this series: Iveragh, Beara and Mizen, and Dingle cover the western end of the range. This book continues with the middle and eastern sections of the range.

These hills in east Munster are rarely as dramatic or savage as their western counterparts, and as a rule they offer easy walking for those new to hill-walking. Many of them can be done as evening walks after tea, and are particularly good fun on a summers evening. As the last glaciation of Munster ended just to the west of Cork city, the hills to the west of this tend to be rougher. In the east, many of the hills are farmed or forested right to the summit.

Local glaciation in the Galty and the Comeraghs developed a series of coums which offer good scrambling possibilities. The rock of the Comeragh is largely conglomerate and found on very few of the other hills in the south. This provides its own very special attractions for hillwalkers, scramblers and climbers.

The Galty and Comeragh also tend to get and hold a lot more snow than their higher counterparts to the west, so winter walking can have particular pleasures for all mountaineers.

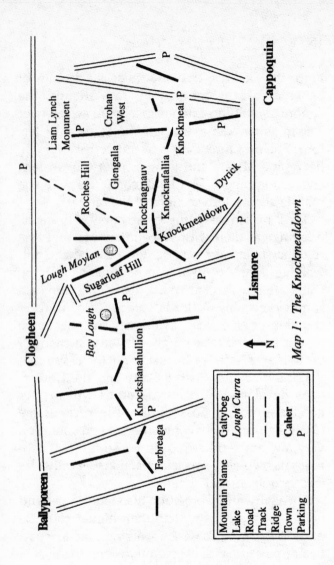

Map 1: The Knockmealdown

Legend:
Mountain Name	Galtybeg
Lake	*Lough Curra*
Road	
Track	
Ridge	
Town	Caher
Parking	P

Towns and features: Ballyporeen, Clogheen, Cappoquin, Lismore

Features: Liam Lynch Monument, Roches Hill, Glengalla, Crohan West, Knocknagnauv, Knocknafallia, Knockmeal, Dyrick, Knockmealdown, *Lough Moylan*, Sugarloaf Hill, *Bay Lough*, Knockshanahullion, Farbreaga

N

18

SECTION I
THE KNOCKMEALDOWNS

The first mountain I climbed was the Sugarloaf hill on the Knockmealdowns, so they hold a special memory for me. These rolling hills are a great introduction to hillwalking, and are very accessible from all over the southeast of the country. The drive through the Vee is one of the finest views in the country, so even if you never got out of your car they are worth a visit. Their main problems are the rampant growth of rhododendron on the lower slopes and a little bit too much conifer planting on the north side of the hills.

Route 1

Mountain group:	Knockmealdown
Route name:	Knocknasculloge
Distance from start to finish:	5.5km
Height gain:	262m
Average time from start to finish:	2.5–3.5 hrs
Starting grid reference:	128068
Map number:	1
Grade:	Hillwalk 1
O.S. 1:50,000 map:	74

1. This is a short easy walk to knock the cobwebs off on a summer's evening. Park at Keane's bridge (128068), situated at the eastern end of the Knockmealdown, and go north up the road on to the broad col. Climb up Knocknasculloge, which is easy, and amble southwest to the boggy col above the source of the Glenshelane river. From here go up Knocknanask, which is a bit steeper, but still no trouble. Descend southeast to pick up one of the mountain tracks leading to the wood, and get back onto the road via a break in the forestry. Go north for 1km to Keane's bridge.

Route 2

Mountain group:	Knockmealdown
Route name:	Glengalla Horseshoe
Distance from start to finish:	17.5km
Height gain:	1115m
Average time from start to finish:	6–7 hrs
Starting grid reference:	077134
Map number:	1
Grade:	Hillwalk 3
O.S. 1:50,000 map:	74

2. Liam Lynch, the commander of the Anti-treaty forces in the Irish civil war, was shot on the slopes of the Knockmealdowns in 1923. This was one of the last acts of that war. His memorial (a round tower) is included in this walk for the sake of the history enthusiast. You can drive to the monument, and start from here but it involves a little bit of uphill at the end of the day, so park at the crossroads to the east of Glengalla bridge (077134). This also makes for a pleasant walk through the wood. Follow any of the boreens south to the East Munster Way, and head east. Don't bother looking too hard for any of the way-markers as the way hereabouts is a little more fiction than fact. You should come across a number of signposts for the monument, and follow these to it (080124). Continue along the upper

track after your visit to the monument, out on to the open mountain, and up to Crohan West. Follow the easy ridge keeping the Knockmealdown wall on your right up on to Knockmeal. Follow the wall southwest from here to Knocknafallia with its ancient cairn on the eastern end. Head west following the wall (which for some reason is not marked on the map) up on to Knocknagnauv. Down then to the col under Knockmealdown where the wall peters out for a while, and then up the steep slope following the wall on to Knockmealdown, with its trig. point. This is readily identifiable by the remains of a multi-channel hut just under the summit. Trundle along north, taking care to avoid the cliff to your right, and, after about 1km, around to spot 768m on your right. Down to Knockshane, keeping the steep ground above Lough Moylan on your left, and down steeply northeast to the track at Roche's Hill. This will lead you down through the wood, on to the road, right back to your car about 1km west away.

ROUTE 3

Mountain group:	Knockmealdown
Route name:	Knockmealdown via Gloungarriff
Distance from start to finish:	8km
Height gain:	731m
Average time from start to finish:	3–4 hrs
Starting grid reference:	066052
Map number:	1
Grade:	Hillwalk 1
O.S. 1:50,000 map:	74

3. Park carefully at Gloungarriff bridge (066052) on the road from Cappaquin over the Vee to Clogheen, and follow the rough track up the mountain by the side of the river on to Dyrick. Wander along east at first, and then up a little steeply on to Knocknafallia. Join the Knockmealdowns wall and head west to Knocknagnauv. The wall was built in the eighteenth century to define the boundary between neighbouring estates. In that time people lived nearly at the top of the hills due to the pressure of population before the famine. As you walk along you will come across old potato beds and shacks quite high up the mountain. Head down to the col under Knockmealdown. If you have had enough, head down the track to Glenakeeffe bridge, and south to your car.

Alternatively, it is up steeply to Knockmealdown which is a real slog. Go back down the broad southwest slope to Glenakeeffe bridge, and along the boreen south to your car.

ROUTE 4

Mountain group:	Knockmealdown
Route name:	Sugarloaf to Knockmealdown
Distance from start to finish:	7km
Height gain:	607m
Average time from start to finish:	2.5–3.5 hrs
Starting grid reference:	031110
Map number:	1
Grade:	Hillwalk 1
O.S. 1:50,000 map:	74

4. Park at the Gap (031110) where there is ample parking, a grotto, a stone pillar which is the grave of a man who wished to be buried upright, a stone shelter, and a nice view. Working out where to go couldn't be easier. Head north along the road from the car park for about 200m and go east uphill towards Glengarriff. Just follow the Knockmealdowns wall east to the summit of Sugarloaf. A rough path has developed on its right side, and it is a little steep. At the summit of Sugarloaf on a windy day you can lean into the east wind at a ridiculous angle as it whips up out of lough Moylan. Keeping the steep ground to your left, head south down to the col, and then up gently to the Knockmealdown plateau. Continue south to the trig. station on the summit of Knockmealdown

with the remains of the television deflector station just under it. Head downhill southwest on easy heathery ground to the Glennandaree stream, and follow this down on a rough patch through the odd clump of rhododendron to the road by an old house at the junction leading down to Lismore. Walk carefully back north along the road to your car. As a short introduction to hillwalking, this is hard to beat.

ROUTE 5

Mountain group:	Knockmealdown
Route name:	Lough Moylan
Distance from start to finish:	7km
Height gain:	631m
Average time from start to finish:	3–4 hrs
Starting grid reference:	044117
Map number:	1
Grade:	Hillwalk 3/Scramble 1
O.S. 1:50,000 map:	74

5. This is a terribly neglected spot despite the fact that a forest track runs right to it. Park at the Vee (044117), and head downhill along the East Munster Way to the stream. A little walking man sign points the way east at the point of the Vee. This is the first hairpin on the way up from Clogheen over the Knockmealdown. Cross this, and go up the other side to the track which heads south into the glen. Continue along this to the lake. Lough Moylan is one of those lakes that appears and disappears depending on water levels and parts of the lake have been overplanted with conifers. Not that this is overly troubling as the only way onward is up. This is a fine spot for lunch unless it is midge season. If you wish, climb the cliff carefully to bring you on to the north summit of Knockmealdown. Swing around the back of the

coum, and head north back along to Sugarloaf hill. Either head west following the wall or continue north downhill to the Vee trying to avoid as much of the rhododendron as you can–good fun except for this. However, the view north to the Galty mountains, and over Clogheen is very pleasant at the end of a short day.

Route 6

Mountain group:	Knockmealdown
Route name:	Sugarloaf to Knockmealdown
Distance from start to finish:	9.5km
Height gain:	870m
Average time from start to finish:	4–5 hrs
Starting grid reference:	031110
Map number:	1
Grade:	Hillwalk 2/3
O.S. 1:50,000 map:	74

6. A fine easy walk whose only drawback is the need for two cars. As you are starting and finishing about halfway up the mountain, it is a great beginners walk. It is of equal difficulty in either direction, but west to east avoids the slog on to Knockmealdown which can be terribly depressing. Park at the grotto (031110) in the Gap, and head up beside the wall to the Sugarloaf. Continue south along the ridge to Knockmealdown, which is easy ground. From Knockmealdown you go down steeply east to the Knockmealdown wall, and up easily to Knocknagnauv. You can either walk along the top of the wall, or follow the track along the side of it which can be a little greasy underfoot. Follow the wall along the flat ridge past Knocknafallia, and around northeast to

Knockmeal where the wall turns north. From Knockmeal you might have to get out your compass in mist. Go east down beside the north end of the wood on to the road at (113084) where your other car should be parked.

ROUTE 7

Mountain group:	Knockmealdown
Route name:	Knockshanahullion
Distance from start to finish:	6–8km
Height gain:	532m
Average time from start to finish:	3–4 hrs
Starting grid reference:	031110
Map number:	1
Grade:	Hillwalk 2
O.S. 1:50,000 map:	74

7. West of the Gap lies Knockshanahullion which tends to get neglected for no good reason. The most logical spot to climb it from is the Gap, but this involves some retracing of steps. Start at the Gap and follow the wall west uphill on to spot 630m above Bay Lough. If you ever needed an explanation as to why the Irish National Parks Service are trying to get rid of rhododendron, the rampant growth around this lake will convince you. From the summit follow the track south, and then west until it peters out under Knock-shanahullion. Go up to the summit, and admire the view. This includes Ballyporeen the ancestral home of Ronald Reagan, and Burnfort, a seventeenth-century towerhouse burnt by the Butlers to stop Cromwell from getting his hands on it. Directly below you, to the northeast, is Clogheen,

where a working smith still shoes horses for the forestry. Off to the north are the Galty mountains. The easiest thing is to head back the way you came. The descent north past the large stone shelter to the rough track along the top of the wood to Bay Lough is also a reasonable option, except for the few steep-sided streams that interrupt your path. Bay Lough is worth a visit on its own from the Gap, so check it out.

ROUTE 8

Mountain group:	Knockmealdown
Route name:	The Towers
Distance from start to finish:	1.5 km
Height gain:	60m
Average time from start to finish:	0.5–1 hrs
Starting grid reference:	025995
Map number:	1
Grade:	Hillwalk 1
O.S. 1:50,000 map:	81

8. This walk has nothing to do with hillwalking other than it involves a little uphill walking. Drive west along the very pleasant north side of the Blackwater from the castle in Lismore. About 2km from the castle is a layby with a signpost for The Towers. Head off up the waymarked track through the tunnel, and round suddenly to the entrance bridge. The best time to visit is on a misty day for the full effect. The best spot for photographs is about 50m up the stream from the bridge. Continue along to the boarded-up gate lodge, and main entrance of the estate, but there is no house to see as it was never built. This is the story. In the eighteenth century, the landowners of Ireland rebuilt their houses in classical style. Lismore castle dates from this period when the Duke of Devonshire, who owned most of this part of

Munster, renovated his home at enormous expense. This set off all the other landowners to improve their estates, and one decided to build a mansion to rival the castle which can be seen from the top of this hill. Unfortunately, their grand plan wiped out the family fortune, and they lived out their days in the gate lodge. To complete the walk continue from the gate lodge down through the trees to the road.

ROUTE 9

Mountain group:	Knockmealdown
Route name:	Knockmealdown Ridge
Distance from start to finish:	20km
Height gain:	1547m
Average time from start to finish:	12–14 hrs
Starting grid reference:	927061
Map number:	1
Grade:	Hillwalk 4
O.S. 1:50,000 map:	74

9. Park at Araglin (927061), which is the point where counties Cork, Waterford, and Tipperary meet. Take the first boreen east out of the village. Then take the first boreen north, and on to the Avondhu way. Go east along this until you can exit out on to Farbreaga. Climb this, and head along to Crow hill before crossing the minor road (983089), and up on to Knockclugga. From here go north to Knock shanahullion for the view. Then go east along to point 630m, before following the wall down to the grotto. This is as good a spot as any to camp.

Head up beside the wall to the Sugarloaf. Continue along the ridge to Knockmealdown. Then go down steeply east to the Knockmealdown wall, and up easily to Knocknagnauv. Sheltering behind the wall here is a good spot for lunch. On then to Knocknafaillia, and around to Knockmeal where the wall turns north. Go south from the summit to Mount Mellary Monastery, and continue down the road to the Youth Hostel. Continue into Cappoquin if you wish. Otherwise come up with interesting ideas as to how you are going to get back to your car!

Section II
The Comeragh and Monavullagh Mountains

The Comeragh are unique in the south of Ireland. They are made of large, rough, gravelly conglomerate and offer a completely different style of climbing to the sandstone mountains of the southwest. From a distance they look like nice, gentle hills. However, there are more horror stories among the southern climbers about these mountains than almost anywhere else, so they should not be taken for granted. In very misty conditions it is a bit like navigating on the top of a snooker table with 150m drops on all sides. It is a scrambler's paradise with no less than 10 coums circling the mountains. These offer some excellent routes at all levels. However, I would advise that you bring (and use) a rope because the large stones that provide your footholds can give without notice. This is not fun if you are standing on them at the time. The mountains are very accessible, and the kind people of Waterford County Council have provided car parking facilities so there is little problem with access. Sadly, this also leads to an incease of thefts from cars so bring your valuables with you or leave them at home. Only the Ordnance Survey call them the Monavullagh mountains' – the rest of us content ourselves with calling them the Comeragh.

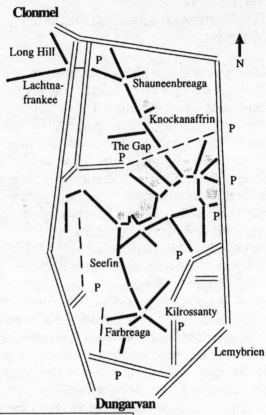

Clonmel

Long Hill

Lachtna-
frankee

P

Shauneenbreaga

Knockanaffrin

P

The Gap

P

P

P

Seefin

P

Kilrossanty

P

Farbreaga

P

Lemybrien

P

Dungarvan

↑ N

Mountain Name	Coumfea
Lake	*Coumtay*
Road	═══
Track	– – –
Ridge	▬▬
Town	**Clonmel**

Map 2: The Comeraghs

ROUTE 10

Mountain group:	Comeragh
Route name:	Farbreaga
Distance from start to finish:	6.5km
Height gain:	260m
Average time from start to finish:	2–2.5 hrs
Starting grid reference:	278019
Map number:	2
Grade:	Hillwalk 1
O.S. 1:50,000 map:	75

10. This is a quick walk after tea with lovely views down over Dungarvan. Park just after Dalligan bridge at the viewing point (278019). Head west for about 50m and take the track uphill to your right. Continue over the easy ground to the shoulder at 494m for a breather. The last 120m of very easy ground bring you to the 'summit' at 617m. The view into the little coum to your east is very pleasant, and the panorama north is of the other Comeraghs. From this summit head south to Farbreaga which is really just the other end of the plateau, before dropping down easily to point 417m. The views south from Farbreaga are of the south coast and Dungarvan Harbour. Descend south through the woods, and then west back along the road to your car – a very pleasant walk.

ROUTE 11

Mountain group:	Comeragh
Route name:	The Tay horseshoe
Distance from start to finish:	14.5km
Height gain:	805m
Average time from start to finish:	5–6 hrs
Starting grid reference:	306048
Map number:	2
Grade:	Hillwalk 3
O.S. 1:50,000 map:	75

11. The Comeragh's Tay river is nothing like its Scottish cousin in the Cairngorms, but the horseshoe is an excellent introduction to the Comeraghs. In truth, you would be best off parking a car at Dalligan bridge (278019), and the other at Mahon Falls (313078). However, if you have only the one, park carefully at Aughatriscar bridge, and follow the boreen west through the woods. At the first junction in the woods go left (south) and out onto the open mountainside. There may be occasional access problems here due to farming requirements. If there are, park carefully by the church in Kilrossanty, (312028), and take the first boreen to your right as you head south. Once you reach the forest at (299028) go left by the side of the wall, and out onto open mountain. Continue uphill by the side of the stream to the shoulder of

Farbreaga with a fine view into the little coum guarding the north side of the hill. Then up steeply to the summit of Farbreaga. Along with the 200m climb on to Seefin, this is just about the total climbing for the day.

Swing around the coum north over Coum-araglin mountain, and down to the col complete with standing stone. This was called Bearna-madree on the old maps, but is not on the new ones. Then go up the long ridge to Seefin. Ignore all modern communications equipment if you can, as it spoils the view. Continue across the EU-funded track coming up out of the Araglin valley, and then across the bog to 715m. As this is practically impossible to find in mist you are better off aiming for the cliffs above Coumtay to its right. Keep these to your right, and use them as a guide rail around to the ridge heading southeast to Comeragh mountain. To your left the cliffs of the Mahon falls could be a problem, so be careful. The ground falls away quite quickly, but the view of the falls to your left is worth any day out. Head south down the 'main road' to your car. In reverse, the walk will avoid any access difficulties, but it is not as nice.

ROUTE 12

Mountain group:	Comeragh
Route name:	The Araglin valley
Distance from start to finish:	15km
Height gain:	608m
Average time from start to finish:	5–6 hrs
Starting grid reference:	263020
Map number:	2
Grade:	Hillwalk 2/3
O.S. 1:50,000 map:	75

12. A quick look at the map will give some idea of how densely populated this area was in ancient times. Ringforts are dotted all around the mountains, and there is a large cluster of archaeological sites on the western side of Seefin. Many of the place names to the north include deer in them, suggesting that food was in plentiful supply in ancient times. Park carefully at (263020) at the southern end of Fabreaga, and follow the track north around the mountain to the first of the stone circles. Off to the south is an ancient grave. Continue along past the old farmhouse to the other stone circle, and then up steeply to the col between Seefin and Farbreaga with its standing stone on the northern end. Head south, yet ignoring the odd bit of modern communications technology and then down west to the track.

ROUTE 13

Mountain group:	Comeraghs
Route name:	Milk Hill to Seefin
Distance from start to finish:	15km
Height gain:	608m
Average time from start to finish:	5–6 hrs
Starting grid reference:	230048
Map number:	2
Grade:	Hillwalk 2/3
O.S. 1:50,000 map:	75

13. Another big long walk, it includes the rarely visited Milk Hill Park at Scart bridge (230048), and follow the boreen north for 3.5km into Coumnagappul. A track on your left leads to the col between Bleantasour 'mountain', and Milk Hill. Go from this col to Milk Hill, and then southeast before swinging north to the summit of Coumfea which stands on a little promontory overlooking the coum. The view into the coum is excellent, especially as the summit is out on a little promontory. Follow the cliff along towards Coumtay, before heading south towards Seefin. Either go down the track just to the north of the summit, or continue south to the col between Seefin and Farbreaga. From here head west down to the wood and the track that leads down to Scart.

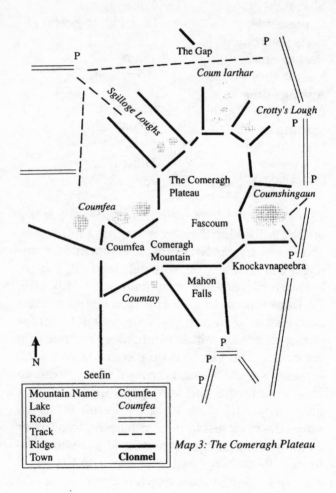

Map 3: The Comeragh Plateau

44

Route 14

Mountain group:	Comeragh
Route name:	Circuit of the Comeragh plateau
Distance from start to finish:	12.5km
Height gain:	732m
Average time from start to finish:	4.5–5.5 hrs
Starting grid reference:	313078
Map number:	2
Grade:	Hillwalk 3/Scramble 1
O.S. 1:50,000 map:	75

14. The most pleasant walk in the Comeragh starts at Mahon Falls which is a great haunt for tourists. Park as you see fit, and go up the ridge to spot 668m in Comeragh mountain. Avoid the vast expanse of bog above the falls, and head west towards Coumfea. The view down into the double loughs of Coumalocha is worth it. Go north from here over point 744m, and continue northward on over point 730m above the Sgilloge Loughs. Go east along the plateau to the small cairn above Coum Iarthar, and then south to the tiny cairn at point 792m. This is known as Fascoum, but the Ordnance Survey have not named it on the new maps. Do not be too troubled if you don't find Fascoum, but do go east from here to have a look at Coumshingaun. This is one of the

most perfect coums to be found in Ireland, or Britain, and sitting at the edge looking down the sheer drop to the lake is a great spot for lunch. Head south along the eastern escarpment down to the shoulder at point 379m. Go down west, steeply at first, to the stream. Wade or hop this as the fancy takes you, and up the steep western bank to the road. Then it's back to your car.

Alternatively, you can climb up beside the Mahon falls which is a very pleasant way up the mountain. The right side of the falls tends to be nicer. The more difficult left side will be no bother to the scrambling brigade. It is also possible to climb the small cliffs to the right of the falls (or nip up one of the small gullies that split them) but these tend to be slimy when wet, so care is needed. This is a great spot for ice climbing when the conditions are right, usually for about three days in February.

ROUTE 15

Mountain group:	Comeragh
Route name:	Circuit of Coumshingaun
Distance from start to finish:	7km
Height gain:	602m
Average time from start to finish:	3–4 hrs
Starting grid reference:	341103
Map number:	2
Grade:	Hillwalk 3/Scramble 1
O.S. 1:50,000 map:	75

15. Coumshingaun is by far and away the most popular walk in the Comeragh, and it is a well deserved popularity. Park at the picnic tables (341103), and follow the track from the northeast corner of this car park. This will bring you to a forest road. Go right along this to a turning circle for forest machinery at the end of the track. A track at the north is partially obscured by bushes, but is obvious once you find it. Follow this over the fence and out on to the open mountain. Go left and follow the fence by the side of the forestry. Two options present themselves:

a. A well worn track leads to the lake at Coumshingaun. Go left uphill to pick up another well worn track on to the arête on the southern side of the coum. The view is marvellous. A track weaves its way through the gendarmes, a series of broken towers, and this will bring you to the back wall of the coum. Alternatively, scramble over them, which is great fun, if a little mossy. Just before the back wall is the high point of the ridge, followed by a gully that drops practically in a straight drop to the lake. There is no way to avoid the short climb up the back wall on to the plateau, but if you follow the track to your left you will discover that it is not difficult. You can also climb directly up from the ridge, but this is very exposed, and of little advantage.

b. An exhilarating, and genuinely scary, scramble can be had by heading directly up the south ridge from the track once it leaves the forestry. Depending on your mood you can go straight up the three buttresses which can be unnerving, but not technically difficult, or drift to your right which is easier, but a little bit mossy. The second buttress is harder, because it is steeper, but is very much the same as the first in rocktype The third buttress is really the start of the arête. Once up these, it is off over the gendarmes, which is no problem after what you have just come up.

After a or b you can head west to point 792m (Fascoum), but it is hardly worth the bother. Instead, follow the lip of the coum to avoid the bog to your left, until the ground begins to fall away towards Iske Sullas. Go right around the lip of the Coum onto the northern ridge, which is a bit scrambley. The view across to the southern arête is particularly impressive from here. Go down this until you are in line with the outfall of the lake, and go down a grassy rake between the cliffs to your right and left. This is a perfect spot to learn the ancient Irish sport of grass glissading, which is great fun. From the lake go back to your car.

ROUTE 16

Mountain group:	Comeragh
Route name:	Coumshingaun east gully
Distance from start to finish:	5km
Height gain:	632m
Average time from start to finish:	2.5–3.5 hrs
Starting grid reference:	341103
Map number:	2
Grade:	Scramble 2/3
O.S. 1:50,000 map:	75

16. In Coumshingaun a large amount of rock climbing has been done on the cliffs. These climbs are covered in Calvin Torrens, *Rock climbing in Ireland*, or Jack Bergin's *The Comeraghs and Southeast*. The hardest crag is the southern one, but the northern one is better because it gets the sun for much of the day. The descent gullies provide good scrambling, and this route is just a sample of the harder stuff to your left, and right. In the northeast corner of the coum a gully falls from the plateau, almost directly to the lake. Follow a sheep track around under the northern cliffs to the base of the gully (323113). Climb up the exposed wall on to the first terrace, and go right for a little to avoid a mossy slab. Climb up to the second terrace. From here the gully narrows in. It is steep,

and a little loose, so great care needs to be taken. A rope is always advisable in the Comeragh, though the climbing may not be terribly difficult. At the top go left, and down over the southern arête.

ROUTE 17

Mountain group:	Comeragh
Route name:	Coumshingaun southwest gully
Distance from start to finish:	5km
Height gain:	632m
Average time from start to finish:	2.5–3.5 hrs
Starting grid reference:	341103
Map number:	2
Grade:	Scramble 2/5
O.S. 1:50,000 map:	75

17. In the southwest corner of the coum, an obvious gully leads up to the south ridge at its highest point. The bottom 50m of the slabs leading up to the gully are hard, and really do require the use of a rope for protection. However, you can avoid all this easily, so it is up to yourself how difficult you want to make it. About halfway up the gully, a large slab bars your way. This has defeated large numbers of scramblers over the years, and is why it gets a grade five. Otherwise its a dawdle. The alternative is to traverse around the obstruction, and then up the gully easily to the narrow col at the western end of the south ridge. Head east over the gendarmes and around down to the lake. Alternatively, you can take the right fork of the gully which leads on to the plateau reasonably

easily. When it snows, these gullies really come into their own, as the sun never hits them. The combination of water ice, and snow makes for a really enjoyable day out.

Route 18

Mountain group:	Comeragh
Route name:	Circuit of Coum Iarthar
Distance from start to finish:	11km
Height gain:	507m
Average time from start to finish:	3.5–4.5 hrs
Starting grid reference:	276128
Map number:	2
Grade:	Hillwalk 3/Scramble 1
O.S. 1:50,000 map:	75

18. While the gap has become a pedestrian motor-way between the Nire valley, and the eastern side of the Comeraghs, very few people know about Coum Iarthar. This is a mistake. Park at the car park in the Nire valley (276128) and follow the marker poles along the track to the gap. Alternatively, park up from the track to Crottys rock and follow the markers leading to the same spot from the east. From here climb up the scrambley ridge on to Carrignagower. This gives you a fine view into the Coum, and its four tiny paternoster lakes. Swing around the back of the coum to the small cairn, and along the flat east side. Then it is down steeply, to the north, before turning left to the low-est lake in the coum. Up from here, and contour around to the gap. The once heather-covered

route is now bare and hard as a result of over-grazing.

Mountain group:	Comeragh
Route name:	Coum Iarthar Arête
Distance from start to finish:	8km
Height gain:	507m
Average time from start to finish:	3–4 hrs
Starting grid reference:	276128
Map number:	2
Grade:	Scramble 5/Rock climbing very severe at least.
O.S. 1:50,000 map:	75

19. While you are never far away from the madding crowds in Coumshingaun, Coum Iarthar is really out in the wilderness. This is a magnificent spot with immense scrambling/rock climbing potential. It is rarely visited, so while some routes have been climbed from time to time there is much to be done here.

Our route begins at the Nire car park (276128), and you follow the track to the gap. Contour around, and descend to the first lake in Coum Iarthar. Follow the stream along to the second, much larger lake. You will pass a deep, mossy gully on your right which is possibly the worst place to go in these mountains. The panorama before you is glorious. You will be immediately drawn to the buttress on your right, topped by a slender pinnacle (314123).

Climbing up the nose of this buttress is potentially one of the best climbs in Ireland, if it can be properly protected. It is outside the range of this guide. Those who are less sure on conglomerate will toddle up the grassy rake to the right of the pinnacle, which brings you almost to the top. Close inspection will show just how broken the pinnacle is, so immense care should be taken when climbing this last 5–10m. It can be climbed by a direct assault from the highest point on to the exceptionally small peak.

Alternatively, you can traverse delicately up the northside of the pinnacle from a few metres down the grassy rake. This will involve a return by the route of ascent. Count to ten, and descend back to the grass, kiss the ground, and promise to be nice to everyone in future! From here go west up the little gully, which is not as easy as it seems and on to the plateau at Carrignagower (point 767m). There are fine views of the upper lake in Coum Iarthar, and the cliffs that guard its upper reaches. Go around the circuit, and down the east ridge with Crotty's rock off on your right. This is another excellent piece of Comeragh conglomerate climbing to frighten the life out of you after Crottys lough.

ROUTE 20

Mountain group:	Comeragh
Route name:	Knockanaffrin ridge
Distance from start to finish:	9km
Height gain:	563m
Average time from start to finish:	3–4 hrs
Starting grid reference:	276128
Map number:	2
Grade:	Hillwalk 3
O.S. 1:50,000 map:	75

20. Park your car at The Gap car park (276128), and head north to the shoulder at point 474m. Cross the 500m letters put on the ground by the Ordnance Survey so you couldn't mistake the mountains (this might not be true), and on up the easy heathery slopes to the pleasant rocky summit of point 630m. The steepness of the east face above Coumduala is a bit of a surprise, given the gentleness of the slope that you have just come up.

You can have a bit of fun on the scrambley 10m eastern escarpment, but the actual moves are difficult enough, so a top rope might be a good idea. A long ramp along the east side under the top of the ridge makes life very easy on a windy day. Otherwise stick to the ridge. As you wander along the ridge to Knockanaffirn, the views of the

58

Suir valley are wonderful. Go down from the summit of Knockanaffrin to the col above Lough Mohra. Continue along the ridge keeping an eye out for a large displaced block on your right, for really intrepid photographs. The suggestion on the O.S. map that the forestry reaches the ridge at the summit of Knocksheegowna is not true. Unfortunately, because the extent of forestry on the 1:50,000 maps is the actual marked land holding, and not the extent of the trees, problems like this will occur from time to time. As a general rule trees peter out at around the 400m level, so you will have to take care when dealing with this. My apologies if you end up fighting through gorse and briars when you expected trees, but these are farmed woods, and constantly changing. Still it is now very easy ground down over Shauneenabreaga, and north northwest towards Powers the Pot (256196), and the T.V. mast just to the south of it. Powers is a spot where every mountaineer should stay. No matter what your budget, from camping to staying in a Bed and Breakfast, Niall Carroll (a former Secretary of the Mountaineering Council of Ireland) will look after you. If you have a moral objection to comfort, go west from Shauneenabreaga, and up on to Lachtnafrankee for the view. Hop into the car you parked hereabouts, and head south along the Comeragh drive to the Nire Valley to pick up your car.

ROUTE 21

Mountain group:	Comeragh
Route name:	Circuit of Coumfea
Distance from start to finish:	11km
Height gain:	595m
Average time from start to finish:	4–5 hrs
Starting grid reference:	276128
Map number:	2
Grade:	Hillwalk 3
O.S. 1:50,000 map:	75

21. In many ways Coumfea is much more spectacular than Coomshingaun, but it is less visited than its eastern neighbour. However, the circuit of Coumfea is one of the nicest, and most rewarding, of the walks in the Comeraghs.

Park at the Gap car park (276128) at the end of the Nire Valley. Go west from the car park, and take a track south which has a signpost for the Sgilloge lakes. Follow this south, and over the Nire until it pretty much peters out beside the stream coming down out of Coumfea. Continue over the boggy ground with good views of the Sgilloge Loughs on your left, before the full extent of Coumalocha and Coumfea appears on your right. Climb up the ridge between the two coums. Once on the flat top of the Comeraghs, head south to point 744m before heading west, and then northwest, up to Coumfea which pokes out from the main ridge like a balcony. The view down here into the coums below is spectacular, and worth the day out on its own. Go west from the summit keeping the cliff on you right, before dropping down along the long ridge to Lyre. Pick up a track to the west of the stream, and cross back to your original track just before its confluence with the stream coming down out of the gap (273125). You can also cross the Nire further west with little difficulty, and follow the road back east to your car.

ROUTE 22

Mountain group:	Comeragh
Route name:	Sgilloge Gully
Distance from start to finish:	10.5km
Height gain:	611m
Average time from start to finish:	3.5–4.5 hrs
Starting grid reference:	276128
Map number:	2
Grade:	Scramble 1/2
O.S. 1:50,000 map:	75

22. At the back of the northern Sgilloge lake (height 501m) a gully leads on to the Comeragh plateau at point 730m. The gully is always wet, very grassy and can be a little slippery at times so care is advised. Some of the higher moves can be a little unnerving, but there are many little terraces to stop on so you have plenty of time to take a break. The view into the coum gets better as you ascend the gully, so relax and enjoy. Keep the rope and a couple of long slings just in case.

ROUTE 23

Mountain group:	Comeragh
Route name:	Coumfea Buttress
Distance from start to finish:	6km
Height gain:	481m
Average time from start to finish:	2.5–3.5 hrs
Starting grid reference:	276128
Map number:	2
Grade:	Scramble 2/3
O.S. 1:50,000 map:	75

23. Park at the Gap car park (276128), and follow the track south over the Nire, just to the west of the car park. Coumfea stands out on a promontory, and it puts down a north ridge to the lakes of Coumlocha. This is a great day out. Go to the lakes under Coumfea, where the north ridge becomes obvious. Climb the fall line with great care, but no unsurmountable difficulty. As with all Comeragh ridges, or gullies, it is advisable to have the rope handy due to mossy and loose rock. Once on top admire the view, and enjoy a well deserved break. Either go west down to Lyre, or around the coum and down the ridge betweem Coumlocha and the Sgilloge loughs towards the Gap.

ROUTE 24

Mountain group:	Comeragh
Route name:	Comeraghs Bog Trot
Distance from start to finish:	26km
Height gain:	1432m
Average time from start to finish:	9–10 hrs
Starting grid reference:	313031
Map number:	2
Grade:	Hillwalk 4
O.S. 1:50,000 map:	75

24. Every year, Niall Carroll and friends organises the Comeragh Bog Trot. This starts in the village of Kilrossanty (313031), and finishes at Powers the Pot. Details are carried in *Mountain Log*. I am not a fan of organised walks, but this is one of the more interesting.

Park carefully by the church in Kilrossanty, (312028), and take the first boreen to your right as you head south. Once you reach the forest at (299028) go left by the side of the wall, and out onto open mountain. Continue up over the small shoulder at point 417m, and to Farbreaga. Then its off over Seefin to the cliffs above Coumtay, where careful navigation is needed. Swing around the back of the Mahon falls on to Knockaunapeebra, the name of which is not marked on the 1:50,000 maps. Strike northeast from here to Coumshin-gaun via point 792m.

Alternatively, you can avoid the bog in the centre of the Comeragh, and skirt around the western cliffs, past Coumfea and the Sgilloge Loughs before heading east to Coumshingaun. The advantage of this detour is that it is much drier than the bog, and probably a little easier to navigate in mist.

Then go northwest to Carrignagower, and down over the scrambley ridge with care to the gap. Up the other side to the Knockanaffrin ridge (route 20), and you're motoring for Powers the Pot.

SECTION III

Slievenamon is the fine easy hill overlooking the valley of the Suir. The view south is one of the finest in Ireland, and the mountain is justifiably made famous by the song of the same name. On the southern slopes is the ruined church and towerhouse of Kilcash, made famous to generations of Irish school students by the poem called Kilcash:

What will we do for timber
The last of the woods is down.

ROUTE 25: SLIEVENAMON

Mountain group:	Slievenamon
Route name:	Slievenamon
Distance from start to finish:	7km
Height gain:	420m
Average time from start to finish:	2–2.5 hrs
Starting grid reference:	317288
Map number:	3
Grade:	Hillwalk 1
O.S. 1:50,000 map:	75/67

25a. The fact that the Ordnance 1:50,000 sheet 75 ends on the southern slopes of Slievenamon is not a problem. It would be a fine walk, if the television people had not bulldozed a track to the summit to put in a mast. Park at the sign for Slievenamon in Kilcash (317288), and follow the track west into the wood. Go south on the track, and out on the open mountainside. Then it's relentlessly north up this track west to the summit ridge. Continue along the track west to the far end with the summit cairn, and television hut. There is a super view of the Suir valley from here, so the trudge is worth it.

25b. A much longer route can be done from the north, but as this would require the purchase of O.S. sheet 67 just for this, I have left it out.

SECTION IV
THE GALTY AND BALLYHOURA MOUNTAINS

Only two mountains outside Kerry reach the magical 3,000-ft Munro mark, despite the fact that any good Scot will tell you that there are no Munros outside Scotland. The first is Lugnaquilla in Wicklow, and the second is Galtymore on the border of Limerick and Tipperary. The Galty dominate the whole south-east of Ireland, and can be seen easily from Cork city over 50km to the south. On a cold clear winter's day with snow you can pick out the Reeks over 80km to the west. These are lovely hills to climb at any time, but really come into their own on a clear night, especially if there is a full moon. As they tend to get and hold more snow than the Kerry hills you can usually manage a great day out. There are no access problems that I know of, but, during lambing, dogs are not welcome on the hills.

The Ballyhouras are an excellent easy introduction to hillwalking. The only real danger is a very cranky red grouse. These hills are normally ignored by hillwalkers due to their low height, but make very pleasant outings after tea.

Map 4: The Galtees

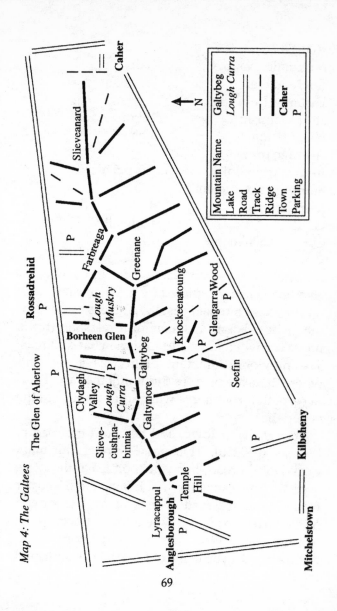

69

ROUTE 26

Mountain group:	Galty
Route name:	Slieveanard
Distance from start to finish:	16km
Height gain:	409m
Average time from start to finish:	4.5–5.5 hrs
Starting grid reference:	030250
Map number:	4
Grade:	Hillwalk 2
O.S. 1:50,000 map:	74

26. The joy of planting acres of acid conifers on acid bog is being explored by the Irish rural communities with mixed results. The eastern end of the Galtees is one vast conifer forest, and this is one place where they add to somewhat dull hills. The previous dominant plant was gorse, and where there are no trees this is still the case. Finding a path through this will add to the joys of the experience.

Start in Cahir town, and head out the road to Lissava (030250). This passes under the main Cork-Dublin road, but you soon leave the noise behind. You can park at Lissava for a shorter walk. At the crossroads here head north to the end of the tarred road, and take a forest track up the hill and over a little ridge. Continue north along this track until you come to a firebreak leading left out on to the open mountainside. Climb up towards the summit via a gap in the forestry plantations, and continue along to Slievenard. Go west to the next col, where yet another track leads downhill south through the woods to the road. Go east past an ancient tomb in the field on your right (worth a look), and back around to Lissava.

ROUTE 27

Mountain group:	Galty
Route name:	Farbreaga and Greenane from the south
Distance from start to finish:	14km
Height gain:	854m
Average time from start to finish:	5–6 hrs
Starting grid reference:	972017
Map number:	4
Grade:	Hillwalk 2
O.S. 1:50,000 map:	74

27. Getting up Farbreaga and Greenane from the south is an easy prospect. It consists of gentle slopes on mountain tracks, which will present no problem to any reasonably fit walkers. A meal in the Kilcoran Lodge Hotel is recommended, as it is a very nice place to spend an hour or two at the end of the day. The greatest danger on this walk comes from the cars on the speedway that doubles as the main Cork-Dublin road. Whatever else you do, keep in by the wall and mind the buses.

Just to the west of Kilcoran wood, a track leads up the mountain to point 631m. Simply hop over the gate, and off you go. The track leads gently through the trees which almost reach the Galty ridge but it is all simple walking country, and in no time at all you find yourself at the ridge. Turning west you continue the rough track along to Greenane, taking care to avoid the cliffs above Lough Muskry to your right. Go west to O'Loughlin's castle, a conglomerate tor eroded in such a way as to look like a battlement. Return to Greenane before going down the southeast ridge. Drop down off this when it levels off to a track on your left through the gorse bushes to Glenyeera wood. A track by the side of the forest leads you back to the main road. Now comes the hard bit!

ROUTE 28

Mountain group:	Galty
Route name:	Galtybeg via Glengarra wood
Distance from start to finish:	14km
Height gain:	820m
Average time from start to finish:	5–6 hrs
Starting grid reference:	930188
Map number:	4
Grade:	Hillwalk 2
O.S. 1:50,000 map:	74

28. Park in Glengarra wood, and follow the forest road up through the specimen trees to the old shooting lodge of Mountain Lodge. This is now an An Óige youth hostel, and is a lovely spot to stay. Cross the bridge here and go north past the wood-shed on your right. This track will lead you to the end of the wood. It zigzags back on itself, and a fire break to your left will lead you out on to the open mountainside. Go left along the side of the wood on a track, and then up to O'Loughlin's Castle which is quite steep. This ridge looks a lot shorter than it is. It levels off at a small outcrop and after three or four of these you reach the main east/west Galty ridge. O'Loughlin's Castle is to your left down in the low point of the col. West along the next hump in the long ridge, and down

fairly sharply to the col above Borheen Lough. From here it is a steep push up the 150m to the summit of Galtybeg. The narrow summit ridge is great fun on a windy day as you make your way to the cairn at the far end. Go south from the summit cairn, and down steeply to the vast expanse of bog that lies below it. Go southeast to make sure that you pick out the Black road, and follow this down to the col under Knockeentoung. Go down steeply east to the Glengarra stream, and follow this down to the wood. Follow the same route back down through the wood to your car. I can recommend doing this as a night walk. All you do is stay in Mountain Lodge, where the main room is so round that the doors are bent. You can hear a whisper on the other side of the room conveyed via the ceiling. Have fun!

ROUTE 29

Mountain group:	Galty
Route name:	The Black Road and Galtymore from the south
Distance from start to finish:	7km/9km
Height gain:	469m/669m
Average time from start to finish:	2.5–3.5 hrs/3.5–4.5 hrs
Starting grid reference:	893203
Map number:	4
Grade:	Hillwalk 2/3
O.S. 1:50,000 map:	74

29a. The ultimate beginners walk is the Black road. The only real dangers are the mossy black stones at the start. Coming from the west, take the next left turn 1km to the east of Skeheenaranky School. Follow this to the end, where a small car park leads east out to the Black road. This peters out just under Galtybeg at a few old turf cuttings. The next section is the only difficult bit as it is quite steep but it really is not very bad. Up this, admire the view, avoid the midge infestation for the month of August, and go back the way you came.

29b. On the other hand if you have discovered a taste for this mountaineering lark then go west from the cairn down fairly steeply to the boggy col between Galtybeg and Galtymore. Jump from peat hag to peat hag, avoid the muck and water, and head up the slope to Galtymore. Finding a dry way is almost impossible. Take care, in mist, of the cliffs above Lough Diheen to your right, but on a sunny day the view into the coum is very pleasant. Up then to Galtymore at 919m, one of Ireland's 'Munros'. The summit cairn and trig. station are at the eastern end of the plateau, but lunch is usually taken a little farther west. Here, at Dawson's Table, is a metal celtic cross, and a small plaque. In cold wintry weather the summit plateau builds up with rime ice. Some of these can be a foot in length, especially on the celtic cross. This makes for spectacular photographs.

The wind on the plateau can be exceptionally strong due to the isolated nature of the ridge, and the fact that it is side-on to the prevailing wind. If you are trying to get to the western end of the plateau in these conditions it is better to drop down under Dawsons Table rather than trying to fight an impossible battle along the top.

The Galty tend to retain their snow cover more than the Kerry hills. This means that you can find the summit of Galtymore covered in ice or snow any time from mid November to early March. It is usually easy enough to crunch your way up or down the slope. In certain conditions the descent of the north side will require crampons, due to its steepness and the many exposed rocks. On the other hand the string of rills that fall 500m from Dawsons Table to the woods provide some of the best glissading territory in the country, without too much likelihood of killing yourself! Super fun, but bring an ice axe, and know how to use it.

Usually, from the summit you go east back to the col, skirt Galtybeg, and pick up the Black road.

ROUTE 30

Mountain group:	Galty
Route name:	Attychraan horseshoe
Distance from start to finish:	14km
Height gain:	899m
Average time from start to finish:	5–6 hrs
Starting grid reference:	879187
Map number:	4
Grade:	Hillwalk 3
O.S. 1:50,000 map:	74

30. The N8 travels in a straight line from Ske-heenarinky school all the way to Cahir. This makes it a lethal stretch of roadway, and it has been the scene of many fatal accidents over the years so take special care. At the school a small side road heads up the hill. Follow this to the pic-nic tables in what used to be Coopers Wood on the old half-inch map, but has no name on the new map (879187). Go up the boreen via the zig-zags, and head north (staying in the wood) up the Atty-chraan valley. At the end of the wood go right uphill to the shoulder at Knocknagalty. From here, head north up the broad slope, and onto the main Galty ridge. Go around right to the summit ridge of Galtymore. The trig. point and cairn are at the other end of the summit ridge. Retrace your steps, and head west to the wall above Lough Curra. Go

west along to Slievecushnabinnia, before heading southwest to Carrignabinnia. If you wish, go west to Lyracappul, for the view of Temple Hill, and Paradise to the west of it. Return to Carrignabinnia. Go down the south-east ridge which is a grand and gentle way off the hill, and up to point 629m. Go down south to pick up a boreen leading down the mountain. Follow this for about 2km, and then go left back to your car at Carrigeen.

Route 31

Mountain group:	Galty
Route name:	Templehill
Distance from start to finish:	10km
Height gain:	899m
Average time from start to finish:	3.5–4.5 hrs
Starting grid reference:	846165
Map number:	4
Grade:	Hillwalk 1
O.S. 1:50,000 map:	74

31. This is known locally by its Irish name, Teampallín. From Kilbelany, go north on any of the boreens to Castlequarter. Park at Castlequarter (846165) and admire the old castle for a while, before going up the boreen to the west. Take either the right or the left fork, and continue out on to the open mountain. You are now on the south ridge of Templehill. The rough track continues up the south ridge which is very easy. It peters out after a while and you continue easily up to the summit. The view east of the other Galtees will give you ideas for other walks, while the views to the west, and south are glorious. You can descend west over Paradise to Anglesborough, or go through the wood southwest by the side of the stream. You will have to wander back along the boreen south to Castlequarter. The easiest thing to

do is to return the way you came. Dead easy, but great fun!

Mountain group:	Galty
Route name:	Anglesborough to Glengarra wood.
Distance from start to finish:	13.5km
Height gain:	1104m
Average time from start to finish:	5–6 hrs
Starting grid reference:	822232
Map number:	4
Grade:	Hillwalk 3
O.S. 1:50,000 map:	74

32. This walk requires the use of two cars, or one friend. Start at the old school in Anglesborough at the western end of the Galty mountains. Follow any of the tracks out on to the open mountain. If you are not sure ask as to the best route. Go straight up towards Lyracappul to a small shoulder overlooking Assaroola glen. This is soul destroying, but it is better than messing around the glen. Continue after a sufficently long rest up to the summit. Follow the ridge east along to Galtymore, with good views north to Lough Curra. Continue down to the col above Lough Diheen, across the peatbogs and up to the narrow ridge of Galtybeg. Then go down to the col above Lough Borheen. Follow the stream south towards Glengarra wood. A sheep track

goes down the east side of the stream. A great spot for a swim is the confluence of our stream with the one coming down off Knockeenatoung.

Down then to the wood about 100m away, and up left to the bend of the wood at (925220). Continue along the wood, and down the firebreak to the main track. Go right, not left, and the track zig-zags back south. This will bring you down to Mountain Lodge. Cross the bridge, and go left down to the main gate of the wood. This is a lovely walk, and the specimen trees to your left and right are named.

ROUTE 33

Mountain group:	Galty
Route name:	Clydagh Valley horseshoe
Distance from start to finish:	8.5km
Height gain:	699m
Average time from start to finish:	3.5–4.5 hrs
Starting grid reference:	875255
Map number:	4
Grade:	Hillwalk 3
O.S. 1:50,000 map:	74

33. From the north the most logical way up Galtymore is via the Clydagh valley. At the Clydagh (875280) Bridge a boreen on the eastern side, just around the bend leads right through the wood. A signpost for Galtymore keeps getting stolen (and seemingly ending up in Irish theme pubs all over the world), but the pole is a useful indicator of where the boreen is. You can park anywhere along this boreen, but it is a bit of a trudge. You can follow this to its end over a ford, and sharp left uphill. You can park off the sharp bend (one car) or on the grass verge halfway up the hill on your right next to an old plough (one car). Alternatively, you can park at the top of the hill by the farmer's house (875255, one or two cars). The 'no dogs' sign really means that, so leave them at home.

Go south along the track to a forestry gate. Go through this out on to the open mountain, and don't forget to close it. You can go left up to Cush from anywhere along the boreen, but from here you might as well aim for Galtybeg. This is a bit of a slog, but it is over soon. From the western end of the summit, go down steeply and wade through the bog, and back up the other side to Galtymore. The summit cairn, and trig. station is at the eastern end of the plateau. Continue along past Dawsons Table, and down the far end of the ridge to the flat ground above Lough Curra. Continue along easily to Slievecushnabinnia. Go down north from here, and then back along the edge of the forest to your car. This is a little boggy underfoot, but gives you a good view of the north side of Galtymore. If you started from the Clydagh Bridge you should take the track on the east side of Slievecushnabinnia back down to the main road a little to the west of your car.

ROUTE 34

Mountain group:	Galty
Route name:	Lough Diheen cliffs
Distance from start to finish:	4km
Height gain:	619m
Average time from start to finish:	2–3 hrs
Starting grid reference:	875255
Map number:	4
Grade:	Scramble 1/2 or Rock 3
O.S. 1:50,000 map:	74

34. The cliffs at the back wall of Lough Diheen attract not only scramblers, but rock climbers as well. At the moment, various friends of mine are trying to force a number of wet routes up the middle of the face, but they tend to be too wet to offer constant good quality climbing. Keep an eye out in *Mountain Log* where more details will appear in due course. On the right side of the Lough a ridge leads up to Galtymore which is a pleasant walk. To the left of this the cliffs can be climbed easily in a series of three to five metre rocksteps, none of which present any great problems. At the top continue to the summit of Galtymore. Descend either down the north side or back over Galtybeg. Great fun, if a little mad.

ROUTE 35

Mountain group:	Galty
Route name:	Lough Diheen gully
Distance from start to finish:	4km
Height gain:	499m
Average time from start to finish:	2–3 hrs
Starting grid reference:	875255
Map number:	4
Grade:	Scramble 1/3
O.S. 1:50,000 map:	74

35. The most interesting gully in the Galty mountains is the one in the south-east corner of Lough Diheen. From the large rock perched on the terminal moraine of Lough Diheen go downhill to the edge of the lake. Follow this around to the south-east corner of the lake. This place is riddled with rabbit warrens so a little care is needed. Pass a gully that peters out halfway up Galtybeg, and go up our gully which is little more than a walk at first. It presents three difficulties. The first is a mossy slab, while the second is a steep wall. Climb the left wall of this to stay out of the stream, and then continue up the gully. The last step before the gully divides can be a little difficult on occasion, but is no real bother. If you wish to make things harder climb the buttress around which the gully divides. This is a little loose, and a couple of

the moves throw you off balance so care is needed. Usually though, you would take the right fork out easily to the boggy ground under Galty-beg.

ROUTE 36

Mountain group:	Galty
Route name:	Lough Muskry Horseshoe
Distance from start to finish:	12.5km
Height gain:	865m
Average time from start to finish:	5–6 hrs
Starting grid reference:	926293
Map number:	4
Grade:	Hillwalk 3
O.S. 1:50,000 map:	74

36. If you feel like it, you can pay a visit to Lough Borheen, which is hidden behind a mass of conifers. It is a pleasant walk and the gully at the back wall offers some possibilities for a scramble. On the other hand the Lough Muskry horseshoe is a much nicer proposition, and is recommended. Park at the Post Office, Shop, Public Phone, and Grotto in Rossadrehid (926293), and head up the boreen going south. Take the first turn on the left over the stream, and then sharp right. Go straight on, and then take the turn on the right which leads you out of the forest. Once out of the forestry, head southeast to Farbreaga. At 724m this is your first vantage point. Continue along the gently rising slope to Greenane at a mere 82m higher. Go down along the ridge to O'Loughlin's

castle which is unnamed on the modern map, but is a well known spot on the mountains. It is not a castle at all, but a conglomerate tor eroded in such a way as to look like a battlement. As such it couldn't possibly be missed. The view north into the coum of Lough Muskry is very pleasant, and this is a fine sheltered spot for lunch.

Continue along the ridge to the next summit with a small cairn, and drop down to the shoulder. Careful navigation is required to make sure that you make the turn for Knockastakeen to avoid the cliffs on your left and right. Once down on the level ground you can make good time to the short rise on to Knockastakeen. Continue north to the forest, and then west to the track coming out of Lough Borheen after about half of a kilometre. Follow the track north to the tarred road, and continue down to Rossadrehid.

ROUTE 37

Mountain group:	Galty
Route name:	Lough Muskry gully
Distance from start to finish:	10km
Height gain:	752m
Average time from start to finish:	3.5–4.5 hrs
Starting grid reference:	926293
Map number:	4
Grade:	Scramble1/2
O.S. 1:50,000 map:	74

37. Park at Rossadrehid. Follow the track south between the grotto and the Post Office. Either go left over the bridge as in walk 36 and follow the track through the forest down to the stream and up the other bank, out onto the open mountain and along to lough Muskry, or go straight on at the bridge to the end of the tarred road, where it goes sharp right. Follow a track with walking markers south from here to join up with the lough Muskry track. Continue to the upper lake. The five perfect echoes that you can get here are almost worth the walk on their own. At the back of the lake an obvious gully splits the cliffs guarding the northern slopes leading to the conglomerate tor called O'Loughlins Castle. This is hard and excellent fun, but our route goes up the gully in the right hand corner of the coum. Climb this which is straight

forward, with a couple of easy rocksteps, but there is a large area of scree at the top of the gully so care is needed. The top of the gully is also threatened by tottering earth columns, but these tend to collapse in little bits rather than large slides so it's not too bad. You arrive at the top of the gully which is only a couple of metres from the tor. Turn left or right as you please. A harder variation involves climbing the cliffs of the coum, which are quite easy but fairly rotten so care is needed.

ROUTE 38

Mountain group:	Galty
Route name:	The Galtees ridge
Distance from start to finish:	29km
Height gain:	1587m
Average time from start to finish:	10–12 hrs
Starting grid reference:	030250
Map number:	4
Grade:	Hillwalk 4
O.S. 1:50,000 map:	74

38. The Galty mountains can be climbed in one long day starting either in Ballydavid wood or Cahir. I prefer Cahir. Start in Cahir town, and head out the road to Lissava (030250). This passes under the main Cork-Dublin road, but you soon leave the noise behind. At the crossroads here head north to the end of the tarred road, and take a forest track up the hill, and over a little ridge. Continue north along this track until you come to a firebreak leading left out on to the open mountainside. Climb up to the summit via a gap in the forestry plantations, and continue along to Slievenard.

Then its off along the winding ridge to Farbreaaga. Turn southwest here to Greenane, and then west to Galtybeg via O'Loughlins Castle. Go down to the col above Lough Diheen, and then up to Galtymore. Head west to Lough Curra. Go west along to Slievecushnabinnia, before heading southwest to Carrignabinnia, and all the way along to Lyracappul. From the end of the narrow summit you go south to Knockaterriff Beg. Unfortunately, to finish the route you have to drop down to the boggy col before Temple Hill. The 185m up here is the most soul destroying that can be imagined at the end of a long day. The delights of Assaroola Glen are an obscene attraction, but for those who stay on the path of righteousness, the pints in Anglesborough will be all the sweeter! However, I think that breaking the walk by staying at Mountain Lodge is a much better idea.

ROUTE 39

Mountain group:	Galty
Route name:	Seefin in the Ballyhouras
Distance from start to finish:	5km
Height gain:	250m
Average time from start to finish:	2.5–3.5 hrs
Starting grid reference:	660181
Map number:	none
Grade:	Hillwalk 1
O.S. 1:50,000 map:	73

39. Looking west from Templehill, a set of low hills guard the other side of the valley north of Mitchelstown. These are the Ballyhouras. They have their own locally-produced map, and a walking route called the Ballyhoura Way. Seefin is the highest point, and can be reached very easily from the orienteering car park in Greenwood. At the moment the O.S. are producing map 73, but you don't really need it. Just go uphill out of the wood, where the only problem is the tangle of brambles which bars your path in some places. On the summit of Seefin is a large shelter. From here go north along the track and over Ballyhoura mountain past the conglomerate tors and T.V. mast to the turning circle. There is a colour-coded map in the turning circle which shows you the

route to your car. The short cut branches off the track at the brow of a hill where there is a sign in blue. This looks very dubious but it leads along the nature trail back to your car. Alternatively just follow the signs for the carpark.

ROUTE 40

Mountain group:	Galty
Route name:	The Comeragh, Knockmealdowns and Galty walk
Distance from start to finish:	104km
Height gain:	3500m
Average time from start to finish:	5–7 days
Starting grid reference:	030250
Map number:	4
Grade:	Hillwalk 5
O.S. 1:50,000 map:	74, 75

40. Start in Cahir town, and head out the road to Lissava (030250). This passes under the main Cork-Dublin road. You can also park at Lissava, but this will mean that you will have to walk back to your car out of Cahir. At the crossroads here head north to the end of the tarred road, and take a forest track up the hill. Continue north along this track until you come to a firebreak leading left out on to the open mountainside. Climb up to the summit, and continue along to Slievenard. Then it's off along the winding ridge to Farbreaga. Turn southwest here to Greenane, and then west to Galtybeg via O'Loughlins Castle. Down to the col above Lough Diheen, and then up to Galtymore. Head west to the wall above Lough Curra. Go

west along to Slievecushnabinnia, before heading southwest to Carrignabinnia, and all the way along to Lyracappul. From the end of the narrow summit you go south to Knockaterriff Beg. Go south from here down to the N8 at Skehenaranky school. There is a large amount of Bed and Breakfast accommodation along the road so you should have no problem finding a bed if you want.

However if you are a lover of kitsch then continue down the boreen to Ballyporeen. This is Ronald Reagan country. You can stay in the Ronald Reagan Bar, eat in the Ronald Reagan Diner, and visit the Ronald Reagan Memorial Toilets constructed for his visit to his ancestral home in the 1980s. If you take a day off you should visit the Mitchelstown caves just up the road. If possible, try and arrange in advance to visit the Earl of Desmond's cave which is a bit more intrepid than the very nice show cave. It is a bit more expensive, but it is worth it.

Leave Ballyporeen and follow the boreen south on to the col to the west of Farbreaga. Climb Farbreaga, and head along to Crow hill before crossing the boreen (983089), and up on to Knockclugga. From here go north to Knockshanahullion for the view. Then its east along to point 630m, before following the wall down to the grotto at the gap. This is as good a spot as any to camp.

Head up beside the wall to the Sugarloaf. Continue along the ridge to Knockmealdown. Then it's down steeply east to the Knockmealdown wall, and up easily to Knocknagnauv. On then to Knocknafaillia, and around to Knockmeal where the wall turns north. Go straight on east to Ballinamult over Knockanask, or go south from the summit to Mount Mellary Monastery, and the Youth Hostel at its entrance.

From the Youth Hostel continue along the boreen to Ballinamult, which also provides Bed and Breakfast accommodation, and a nice pub. Leave Ballinamult, and cross the main Clonmel to Dungarvan road. You then cross another main road, and go north to the bottom of Milk Hill.

From Milk Hill, follow the ridge southeast and then north to Coumfea. The view into the coum is excellent especially as the summit is out on a little promontory. Follow the cliff along towards Coumtay, and go along the edge of the plateau beside the Sgilloge Loughs. Then go northeast to Carrignagower, and down over the scrambley ridge with care to the gap.

Head up the easy heathery slopes to the rocky summit of point 630m. The steepness of the east face above Coumduala is a bit of a surprise given the gentleness of the slope that you have just come up. You can have a bit of fun on the scrambley 10m eastern escarpment, but the actual moves are difficult enough, so a top rope might be a good idea. A long ramp along the east side under the top of the ridge makes life very easy. As you wander along the ridge to Knockanafrin, the views of the Suir valley are very pleasant. Down from the summit of Knockanaffrin to the col above Lough Mohra. Continue along the ridge keeping an eye out for a large displaced block on your right, for really intrepid photographs. The suggestion that the forestry reaches the ridge at the summit of Knocksheegowna is not true. It is easy ground down over Shauneenbreaga, and north northwest towards Powers the Pot (256196). From here head down to Clonmel, and get the rare train to Cahir.

Hillwalks and Scrambles by Degree of Difficulty

Hillwalk 1	Knocknasculloge
Hillwalk 1	Knockmealdown via Gloungarrif
Hillwalk 1	Sugarloaf to Knockmealdown
Hillwalk 1	Lough Moylan
Hillwalk 1	The Towers
Hillwalk 1	Farbreaga
Hillwalk 1	Slievenamon via the Multichannel track
Hillwalk 1	Temple Hill
Hillwalk 1	Seefin in the Ballyhouras
Hillwalk 2	Knockshanahullion
Hillwalk 2	The Slievenaman ridge
Hillwalk 2	Slivenard from Cahir
Hillwalk 2	Farbreaga and Greenane from the South
Hillwalk 2	Galtybeg via Glengarra wood
Hillwalk 2/3	Sugarloaf to Knockmeal
Hillwalk 2/3	The Araglin valley
Hillwalk 2/3	Milk Hill to Seefin
Hillwalk 2/3	Galtymore via the Black Road
Hillwalk 3	The Circuit of Coum Iarthar
Hillwalk 3	The Tay Horseshoe
Hillwalk 3	Glengalla Horseshoe
Hillwalk 3	The circuit of the Comeragh Plateau
Hillwalk 3	The circuit of Coumshingaun
Hillwalk 3	Knockanaffrin Ridge
Hillwalk 3	Circuit of Coumfea